Copyright © 2016 by Sherria L. Elliott

Written by Sherria L. Elliott

Illustrated by Sasha Moore

All rights reserved.
Published by 4Elliott Publishing, Inc.
Heaven and associated characters, logos, trademarks and design elements are registered, owned and licensed
by
4Elliott Publishing, Inc. and Sherria L. Elliott © 2016

No part of this publication may be reproduced, stored in a retrieval system, or transmitted in any form or by any means, electronic,
mechanical, photocopying, recording, or otherwise without written permission of the publisher.

For information regarding permission, write to:
4Elliott Publishing, Inc.
Attention: Permissions Department
16759 SW 16th St, Pembroke Pines, Fl 33027
Email to: 4Elliottpublishing@gmail.com or call: 786-277-2693
www.4Elliottpublishing.com

ISBN: 978-0-9846963-3-8

Library of congress cataloging Publication Data Pending
Manufactured in the United States of America.

The *But Mommy It's Not Fair!* series is dedicated to my daughter Sheterria "Heaven" Elliott. Your diligence to make kids understand who you are has been my driving force to help you make a difference in this world. You are my shining light and I love you to the moon and beyond.

♥ Love, Mom ♥

A special "Thank you" to my eldest son, Terry Jr. Learning to understand "Albinism" yourself, and seeing your sisters' struggles had to be hard on you at such a young age. Thank you for being the best big brother she could have. I love you, son.

This book belongs to:

_____

Aisle 7

Pens
Pencils
Markers
Erasers
Crayons

Notebooks

Heaven went school shopping with her mom, but she wasn't as excited as usual. She was going to start Middle School tomorrow at a new school and with new friends. Meeting new people always made her afraid.

Her mom noticed her mood and asked
Heaven why she looked so sad.

"I'm not excited to be going to a new school
mommy!" she said. "All I can think about is
when I started Pre-k and all the kids stared at
me because I was different."

Her mom started to remember that day like it was now. Heaven couldn't get that day out of her head. They both stood silent in the store, thinking.

Heaven could hardly contain herself as they drove to school. "I'm so excited mommy!" she would say.

Finally at school, she entered her class, but was soon aware that all the kids stopped what they were doing to look at her.

Feeling uneasy, Heaven put her head down, wanting to disappear from their stares. She had no idea why everyone was staring at her.

Although she is African-American, Heaven was not the same color as her parents. She was born with a genetic condition called "Albinism", which is little color or no pigment in her hair, skin, and eyes.

Because she has pretty blonde hair, soft milky skin, and dazzling grey eyes, she looks Caucasian or "white."

Her different skin color is something she had never thought about before because her parents showered her with so much love. Now she saw a difference.

Heaven ran to her parents in tears. "But mommy it's not fair!" she would say. Distraught, she wanted to go back home.

Although this broke her parents' heart, they had to explain to her that, "Kids just don't understand."

16

Her parents took her aside to help her understand some things. The kids had never seen such a unique person like her. They wanted to know why she looked different than them, and they wanted to know why she looked different than her parents. Her parents told her this was very confusing to the kids, and difficult for them to understand.

Heaven's dad decided to make a game for the kids to answer their questions.

"Is that your mom and dad?" asked a little boy.
"Are you white?" asked another.
Why do you have blonde hair?"

Heaven was scared at first, but while holding onto her daddy's hand, she slowly answered their questions and began to feel better.

When the last little girl asked her, "Can we be friends?" Heaven looked at her parents and smiled the biggest smile ever! "I'm ok now!" she would say.

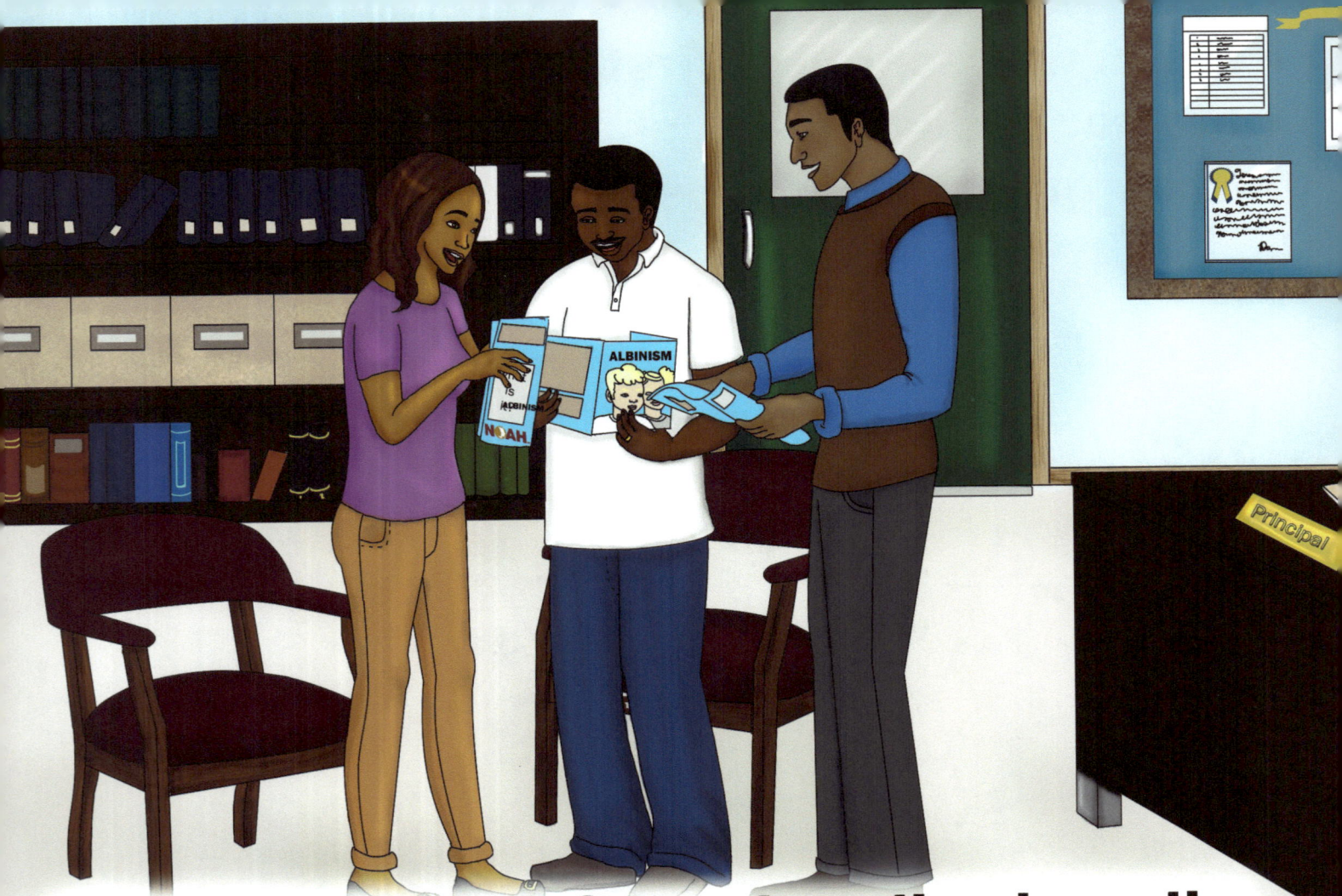

After her parents left her class, they knew they had to get the school involved with informing teachers, parents, and kids about "Albinism." This was the only way they could make kids understand and ensure Heaven would have a great school year.

By the end of the day she had made so many friends that Heaven's, "But mommy it's not fair!" had turned into, "They all understand now, mommy!"

Her mom finished her thoughts, then asked Heaven, "Once the kids knew what 'Albinism' was, you made new friends, right?"
"Yes mom," said Heaven.

Her mom then let Heaven know that she can't be afraid to go to a new school or meet new people because she is different.

She had to be willing to face people and explain Albinism to them, because a lot of people just don't know. She was going to middle school now, and she had to help them understand who she was.

Heaven smiled and said, "I love you mom, now I'm ready for middle school!"

Now, if every parent would explain to their kids how people come in all shapes, colors, and sizes, then Heaven and any other girl or boy who has "differences" could live happily ever after.

The End

The moral of Heaven's story is that helping kids to understand the answers to their questions helps them move on to meaningful friendships.

Helping kids understand

Helping kids understand

www.ingramcontent.com/pod-product-compliance
Lightning Source LLC
Chambersburg PA
CBHW040023050426

42452CB00002B/107